Also by Alex J. Goldman

GIANTS OF FAITH: GREAT AMERICAN RABBIS
THE QUOTABLE KENNEDY

The
Truman
Wit

H.S.

edited by ALEX J. GOLDMAN

WITHDRAWN

The Citadel Press   *New York*

E 814 .A37 1966

Truman, Harry S., 1884-1972.

The Truman wit

Wide World Photos

Contents

Introduction

In a note to his daughter Margaret, Harry Truman once wrote, "Your dad will never be reckoned among the great, but you can be sure he did his level best and gave all he had to his country. There is an epitaph in Boothill Cemetery in Tombstone, Arizona, which reads, 'Here lies Jack Williams; he done his damndest.' What more can a man do?"

Many millions will strongly disagree with Harry Truman's modest estimate of his service to his country. They will disagree and call him great—a man of decision and a forthright and fearless President.

Harry Truman has always identified intimately and easily with the American people. He feels himself to be one of them, and his ready wit, sharp repartee, and home-spun humor have brought him close to the thousands who have milled around railroad stations and elsewhere to hear him.

Collected here are examples of Harry Truman's incisive wit and humor. Here is Mr. Truman at his best—in the Congress, as Vice-Presidential and Presidential candidate, as President, and as private citizen. And here, too, are samples of the *original* Truman wit—remarks by Mrs. Martha Truman, the President's mother. Thoroughly motherly and practical in her outlook, Mrs. Truman's remarks—typically American, warm, and lively—constitute a humorous commentary on her son's political career.

The selections presented here reflect the dignity and the simplicity of the thirty-third President of the United States, who succeeded Franklin Delano Roosevelt in one of history's most crucial years and led America to peace, with strength.

ALEX J. GOLDMAN

In the Senate

At a banquet in St. Joseph, Missouri, attended by a number of judges, a master of ceremonies called the Judiciary the most important branch of the government. Mr. Truman "corrected" the speaker:

"The legislative is! It's close to the people and provides the money to run the government. I can say anything I want to about judges, because I have no license to practice law. Therefore, no license can be taken away from me. Besides, I can't be sued, because I haven't anything."

Huey Long, of Louisiana, known as the "Kingfish," was a long-winded speaker. Mr. Truman, who had been asked by Vice-President John Nance Garner to chair a Senate session, recognized the southern Senator. When Long rose to speak, many of his colleagues left the chambers, leaving Mr. Truman with a small number of Senators. True to pattern, Long spoke for hours. When the long tirade was over and Long walked across the street with Senator Truman, he turned to the unhappy chairman, and asked, "What did you think of my speech?"

"I had to listen to you," Senator Truman replied, "because I was in the chair and couldn't walk out."

"I'm content just where I am. I'm happy in the Senate. I have friends and I don't have any political ambitions. You know, people call me a politician, and you know the way some say it. Well, you've got to be a politician in the first place to get to be a Senator. When you're dead, they call you a statesman. . . ."

Chairing a Senate session on another occasion, Mr. Truman spotted former Senator Prentiss Brown of Michigan listening at the back of the chamber. He summoned a page, jotted down the following note, and sent it to the distinguished guest:

"Dear Prentiss. Ain't it hell? We're both muzzled now. You have my sympathy. Harry."

In 1944, when Senator Truman was asked whether he had considered running for Vice-President, he said:

"I don't want to be Vice-President. I bet I can go down on the street and stop the first ten men I see, and that they can't tell me the names of two of the last ten Vice-Presidents of the United States."

The Vice-Presidency

Listening to the election returns, 1944.

Noticing how spirits were sinking as early election results indicated a loss for the Vice-Presidential candidate, Mr. Truman rushed over to a piano, called out: "I think that this calls for a concert," and proceeded to play Paderewski's Minuet.

November 7, 1944

Speaking to a newsman who had not supported him during the campaign, Vice-President Truman said:

"A strawman has been constructed that you newspapers will now have to bury. Nobody told me how to do my duty, and I feel that I have served the people. But I never forget a favor. If I had been willing to forget my friends, I could have had headlines in your damn paper and plenty of other papers."

November 8, 1944

During President Roosevelt's last days, Vice-President Truman joined some Congressmen on a boating expedition.

"You guys have a fifteen-thousand-dollar-a-year oarsman," Mr. Truman remarked as he rowed.

Standing up to relieve the cramping of his body on the return trip, the Vice-President was hurled into the cold waters as the boat suddenly lurched forward.

After being pulled out, Mr. Truman sat in the corner of the boat, shivering beneath some heavy blankets. He called out to Sam Rayburn, "You just go on and catch the fish, Sam, and I'll do the swimming."

Mr. Truman with President Franklin D. Roosevelt in 1944.

The Presidency

1945—1948

Don't be unbrotherly
Brother

The day Harry Truman assumed the Presidency, following the death of Franklin Delano Roosevelt, he spotted newsmen outside Senate Secretary Biffle's office. Modestly, he went to each, shook hands all around, and asked:

"Did you ever have a bull or a load of hay fall on you? If you have, you know how I felt last night. I felt as if two planets and the whole constellation had fallen on me. I don't know if you boys pray, but if you do, please pray to God to help me carry this load."

Soon after he became Chief Executive, Mr. Truman called Secretary of Commerce Jesse Jones to inform him that "the President has sent John Snyder's name to the Senate for confirmation as Federal Loan Administrator."

"Did the President make that appointment before he died?" Jones asked curtly.

"No," retorted Mr. Truman, "he made it just now."

"Some Senators and Congressmen come in and pass the time of day, and then go out and help me save the world in the press."

June, 1945

Before he became Vice-President, Mr. Truman joined Sam Rayburn for a week-end of fishing, during which he was "accidentally" spilled into the creek. He sat dangling from the boat for a while, managing to keep his feet inside the boat and his head above water.

When he became President, he quipped, "Can you imagine me now, taking sixteen Secret Service men, telephone and telegraph connections, representatives of three press associations, radio, photographers, and special writers on a personal excursion of that sort? And then let something like that happen."

Governor Wallgren of the state of Washington once visited Mr. Truman at the White House. He mentioned that a Seattle newspaper editorial regarded him as a Presidential possibility.

That afternoon, the Governor accompanied the President to the White House swimming pool. As soon as the President edged near the pool, six Secret Service men appeared as if from nowhere and began hovering about him.

The President turned to Governor Wallgren, and said, "See? You don't want this job."

**The President and his First Lady enjoy a laugh
at the National Press Club in 1945.**

Mr. Truman tells the story of the time Stalin gave a dinner for dignitaries attending the Potsdam Conference:

"All the Russians were drinking a lot of vodka. Stalin kept pouring all night from a special bottle he had in front of him and drinking one drink after another. Finally I asked if I could taste what he had in that bottle. You know, it was nothing but a light French white wine?"

Mr. Truman's frankness is legendary, no matter the person or subject involved. In a discussion with Vyacheslav Molotov, Mr. Truman declared that the United States would gladly carry out its agreements reached at Yalta, but insisted upon mutual observation of those agreements.

Mr. Molotov, stunned by the sharpness of the President's remarks, said, "I have never been spoken to like that in my life."

"Carry out your agreements and you won't get talked to like that," retorted the President.

July, 1945

"At Potsdam one day, after a meeting, I took Fred up to Stalin and I said, 'Marshal Stalin, I want you to meet Marshal Canfil.'

"Of course, I didn't tell him Fred was only a Federal marshal in Missouri and not a military marshal."

In August, 1945, Mr. Truman visited England as the guest of King George VI. When the band leader struck up the American national anthem on the last day of his visit, Mr. Truman turned to the king, and said, "Your Majesty, I want to get that man to teach our bands how to play 'The Star-Spangled Banner!' "

Commenting on his daughter's hobby of taking photographs in the White House, Mr. Truman said:

"It's not enough that my homely countenance is at the mercy of the press—I have to have a photographer in the family."

We have found that it is easier for men to die together on the field of battle than it is for them to live together at home in peace.

December 24, 1946

Wars are different from baseball games where, at the end of the game, the teams get dressed and leave the park.

April, 1946

Stepping up to the podium to deliver the State of the Union message, the President looked over the members of both Houses of Congress. Before beginning his speech, he remarked:

"It seems to me a lot of you moved over to the left [Republican] side since I was here last."

January, 1947

Harry Truman's quick tongue often brought stinging rebukes. On one occasion in 1947, the President's corresponding secretary, Bill Hassett, informed Mr. Truman that the rector of an exclusive Washington church had stated that he would have spoken as the President had under similar provocation. The President's face lighted up, but after a few seconds he frowned.

Remembering a personal incident, he said glumly, "I wish that the rector would go talk to my wife."

Sitting with friends in Caruthersville, Missouri, President Truman was prevailed upon to play Paderewski's Minuet.

He walked over to the piano, sat down, and before he began to play, turned to his audience, and said, "When Stalin heard me play this, he signed the protocol."

October, 1945

Tripping over his academic gown at Princeton's Two-Hundreth Anniversary Celebration, the President blurted out:

"Whoops! I forgot to pull up my dress."

June, 1947

In 1947, the Freedom Train's cross-country tour gave thousands of people an opportunity to see some of the nation's historical documents firsthand.

When the train stopped at Union Station in Washington, D.C., President Truman went to see the exhibition. Reading General Washington's army supply accounts, he mumbled audibly, "Rum on every page."

President Truman's suggestion that a balcony be added to the White House was opposed by the Fine Arts Commission. Ignoring the Commission's decision, the President explained that the South Portico had been designed by Thomas Jefferson and that the original plans called for a balcony.

"All changes in the White House since Fillmore's time have faced resistance—like gaslights and cooking stoves. Mrs. Fillmore put in the first bathtubs, and she was almost lynched for doing it."

Remarking on the success of his visit to Brazil in September, 1947, President Truman said:

"We have never had such a reception. I am tempted to come and run for Mayor of Rio de Janeiro—and I think I could be elected."

Headed for his mother's home in Grandview, Missouri, President Truman telephoned his sister from the Presidential plane, and said:

"Tell her I'm about a mile and a half from St. Louis— straight up."

March, 1947

A scolding for the Republicans.

Speaking before the National Conference of Editorial Writers, Mr. Truman chided:

". . . there are a great many instances where editorials are mailed to me from out of town. . . . I get up before daylight every morning—I have the reveille habit—and I spend a good part of that time going over all the Washington papers and the New York papers, Baltimore *Sun,* Philadelphia *Bulletin,* and many others that I have time to read. But I read them myself because I like to read them.

"And I find out lots of things about myself that I never heard of."

October 17, 1947

In December, 1947, President Truman sat down to note his reactions to the many questions asked about his health, and to explain how he was able to avoid unnecessary tensions, anxieties, and problems.

He wrote that he was a firm believer in exercise, walking and swimming in particular, and that he was blessed with the capacity to brush aside undue cares.

With tongue in cheek, he noted that he had appointed a "Kitchen Cabinet" of special assistants to do the worrying for him in areas in which he thought he should not become involved. He had selected a Secretary of Inflation to convince people that despite any inflationary flight of prices no inflation existed in fact and there was no need for concern; a Secretary of Reaction to put the atom back together so that international relations would improve and tension between the United States and the Soviet Union would be eliminated; a Secretary for Columnists to analyze the words, ideas, and criticisms of all the columnists and submit to the President the distilled essence of all suggestions as to how to run the country and the world; and a Secretary of Semantics to supply him with long words for his speeches, to teach him how to be diplomatic, how to say yes and no in the same breath without fear of contradiction, and how to say one thing in one city and the opposite at the other end of the land, while creating a sense of unity.

In 1947, the President moved his family out of the White House while two cracking floor beams were under repair. He commented:

"My heart trembles when I think of the disasters we might

have had with sixteen hundred people at those White House receptions, none of them knowing that the hundred-and-eighty ton roof might fall on their heads at any moment.

"The only thing that kept the White House up was habit."

A severe storm struck one day in March, 1948, when Mr. Truman and some guests were aboard the Presidential yacht. Although many of the guests took sick as the boat tossed about, President Truman maintained his strength.

As he explained, when they docked at the naval base in Guantanamo, Cuba, "I stood up all right for the simple reason that I didn't get up. I stayed in bed."

"The life expectancy of the human man in Caesar's time was thirty-one years. It is now over sixty—I think sixty-two. If we keep that up, we will all be so old that we will join the Townsend Plan* and be paying taxes to keep each other in pensions so we can live forever."

May 1, 1948

Attending a dinner for a small group of important politicians in Chicago, Mr. Truman reminisced:

"In earlier years, I came to Chicago on shopping trips with Mrs. Truman. I enjoyed looking in the windows. No one paid any attention to me then. I suppose a lot of

*The Townsend Plan (1933) proposed an old-age pension to be financed by a 2% Federal sales tax.

people wish I was looking in windows again. But they won't get their way, because a year from today I'm going right back to the same trouble I'm in now."

June, 1948

Mr. Truman's widely-publicized cross-country non-political trip in 1948 took him to Santa Barbara, California, on June 14 at 7:15 A.M. He greeted his audience by remarking:

"It is a little too early in the morning to make a real political talk, or a non-political talk, because this is supposed to be a non-political trip. That all depends on your viewpoint. If you are on my side, it's non-political; if you are not, it's a low-down political trip, to come out and tell the people what they ought to hear."

Humor aboard the campaign train, 1948.

Typically Truman: A speech from the rear platform of a campaign train.

When he arrived in San Bernardino, Mr. Truman was presented with a basket of eggs.

"At least they didn't throw them at me," he remarked.

June, 1948

At a train station in Barstow, California, a woman called out to President Truman, who was standing on the rear platform, "President Truman, you sound as if you have a cold."

The President bounced back, "That's because I ride around in the wind with my mouth open."

When he accepted the Democratic Presidential nomination, Mr. Truman "poured it on" the Republicans:

"Herbert Hoover once ran on the slogan: 'Two cars in every garage.' Apparently the Republican candidate this year is running on the slogan: 'Two families in every garage.' "

July, 1948

During the 1948 Presidential campaign, Mr. Truman summoned the Republican-controlled Congress back to Washington and challenged it to action. Speaking from the rear platform of a train, he jibed:

"Now, my friends, if there is any reality behind that Republican platform, we ought to get some action from a short session of the Eightieth Congress. They can do this job in fifteen days, if they want to do it. They will still have time to go out and run for office."

July, 1948

"My opponent is conducting a very peculiar campaign. He has set himself up as a kind of doctor with a magic cure for all the ills of mankind.

"Let's imagine that we, the American people, are going to see this doctor. It's just our usual routine check-up which we have every four years.

"We go into the doctor's office.

" 'Doctor,' we say, 'we're feeling fine.'

" 'Is that so?' says the doctor. 'You been bothered much by issues lately?'

" 'Not bothered, exactly,' we say. 'Of course, we've had quite a few. We've had the issues of high prices, and housing, education and social security, and a few others.'

" 'That's bad,' says the doctor. 'You shouldn't have so many issues.'

" 'Is that right?' we say. 'We thought that issues were a sign of political health.'

" 'Not at all,' says the doctor. 'You shouldn't think about issues. What you need is my brand of soothing syrup—I call it "unity." '

"Then the doctor edges up a little closer.

" 'Say, you don't look so good,' he says.

"We say to him, 'Well, that seems strange to me, Doc. I never felt stronger, never had more money, and never had a brighter future. What is wrong with me?'

"Well, the doctor looks blank, and says, 'I never discuss issues with a patient. But what you need is a major operation.'

" 'Will it be serious, Doc?' we say.

" 'No, not very serious,' he says. 'It will just mean taking out the complete works and putting in a Republican Administration.'

"That's the kind of campaign you're getting from the Republicans. They won't talk about the issues, but they insist that a major operation is necessary."

"This year the same candidate is back with us, and he is saying much the same thing; that he likes our Democratic laws, but that he can run them better than we can.

"It sounds like the same old phonograph record; but this year the record has a crack, and the needle gets stuck in it. The crack was provided by the Republican Eightieth Congress.

"In 1948, every time the candidate says, 'I can do it better,' the crack says, 'We're against it.'"

"In 1940, the Republicans had a poll that told them they had the edge. Well, it was a mighty sharp edge. They got cut to ribbons on election day."

"These polls are like sleeping pills designed to lull the voters into sleeping on election day. You might call them 'sleeping polls.'

"The same doctor I told you about the other night in Pittsburgh—the Republican candidate—keeps handing out these sleeping polls, and some people have been taking them. This doctor keeps telling the people: 'Don't worry. Take a poll and go to sleep.'

"But most of the people are not being fooled. They

know that sleeping polls are bad for the system. They affect the mind. An over-dose could be fatal."

"I want to read you something here that is just as interesting as it can be—I don't think I have ever seen anything as interesting. Now, this is called *The Republican News.* It is the official publication of the Republican Party. Now, I want to read you something because it is very enlightening. It is exceedingly enlightening, and it is terrible for the country.

"Here it is: 'Don't Throw Peanuts to the Elephant!' Wait a minute—you will find out what the 'peanuts' means. Take a look: 'Many of our friends feel that, entirely apart

The President and Winston Churchill depart for Fulton, Missouri, where Churchill was to make his famous "iron curtain" speech.

from other important considerations, the least they can do to express their appreciation is to contribute a substantial part of their tax savings for this year to insure the re-election of the Congress which made this possible.'

"That is the terrible Eightieth Congress they are talking about, that didn't do anything for the country."

"Don't let the Republicans fool you with their smooth talk about what they are going to do for the farmers and the workers and the small businessmen of this country.

"Their actions speak louder than words. You know, Uncle Joe Cannon had quite a career in this great town [Danville], and he was present when one of your colleagues said he would rather be right than President. Old Uncle Joe made a famous answer. He said: 'I am sure that my worthy friend will never be right, or President either.'

"I think that is absolutely true of the Republicans today. They will never be right, and they will never elect a President if the people understand what they are trying to do."

"And when I think of the New Deal and all that it meant, I can't help but think of another dinner that was held in the Waldorf about a year ago. That dinner was held to honor the fifty foremost business leaders. The publicity about that dinner was very careful to point out that the combined income of those fifty foremost business leaders was $7,500,000 a year! That's an average of $150,000 a year for each one of them.

"Now, at every dinner like that they must have a speaker. They looked around for a speaker who would be able to talk the language of those who make $150,000 a year. They didn't ask me.

"But they didn't have a great deal of trouble finding a man who would. He was practically within whistling distance—it's about 150 miles from here to Albany. So they whistled, and the speaker hurried right down here. He was anxious to make a name for himself—because he wants to be President.

"Right here in the Waldorf-Astoria, he rose up before the assembled millions—dollars, not people—and began his speech. This is how he started: 'Fellow victims of the New Deal.' Believe it or not, this man thought it was funny to call the $150,000-a-year men 'Fellow victims of the New Deal.'

"I really don't think those men had much to complain about. I think they fared very well under the New Deal."

"Not long ago, an elderly man who was driving into Gary gave a lift to a young man going his way.

"During their talk, the older man asked the young fellow, 'What takes you to Gary?'

"The young man hesitated, put his head down, and said: 'I am working for the Republican State Committee. They are sending me to Gary to see what I can do to get the people there to vote the Republican ticket.'

"The old man was silent for a while, and then he said: 'Son, I've listened to sad stories for fifty years, and that's the saddest one I've heard yet.'

"I agree. I can think of no harder job than to try to

**At the Democratic National Convention in Phila-
delphia, Mr. Truman poses with his running mate,
Alben W. Barkley, and Mr. Barkley's daughter,
Mrs. Max Fruitt. Mrs. Truman is at the left and
Margaret Truman at the right.**

sell the Republican Party to the men and women of Gary
who lived through those dark years of the Republican
depression in 1930, 1931, and 1932."

"What did the Republicans do with my proposal for
health insurance? You can guess. They did nothing.

"All they said was: 'Sorry. We can't do that. The medical
lobby says it's un-American.'

"The Governor of the state of New York now wants to
be President. He was asked right at the height of the

fight in Congress what he thought about the Taft-Ellender-Wagner Bill. Do you know what he said? He said, 'I haven't had time to read it.' Well, he pretends to know something about housing, but if he's too busy to read the bill that would have made the difference between houses and no houses, then he doesn't know much."

"The other day, a cartoonist for a Republican newspaper drew a cartoon of me that I enjoyed. He showed me dressed up as Paul Revere, riding through a colonial town, yelling to the townspeople: 'Look out! The Republicans are coming!'

"It was a good cartoon. There's a lot of truth in it. But it's not quite accurate. What I am really telling you is not that the Republicans are coming, but that they are here. They have been in Washington for the last two years in the form of the notorious Republican 'do-nothing' Eightieth Congress."

September 20, 1948

"I am trying to fix it so the people in the middle-income bracket can live as long as the very rich and very poor. . . ."

Asked by Bartly Crum, publisher of the New York *Star,* why he had decided to run for the Presidency, Mr. Truman looked around his Presidential office, and replied: "Where would I ever find another house like this?"

September, 1948

President Truman reminisced about his attempt to enlist during World War II:

"The General [George Marshall] pulled down his specs on the end of his nose, like that, and said, 'How old are you?' I said, 'Well, I am fifty-six.'

" 'Well,' he said, 'you are just too old for this one. This is a young man's war. You had better go back and do your duty in the Senate.'

"And I went back and did the best I could in the Senate, and you see where I got myself by doing it.

"Then General Marshall afterwards, as Chief of Staff, was sitting out in my office one day to see me, and my Secretary, Mr. Connelly, asked him what his reply would be under the circumstance he then labored under, when I was President and he was Chief of Staff.

" 'Well,' the General said, without batting an eye, 'I would make the same answer, but I would be a little more diplomatic about it.' "

September 21, 1948

At the start of one of the extended whistle-stop campaign trips, Alben Barkley went to Union Station to see the President off.

When the train was about to depart, the Vice-Presidential candidate encouraged Mr. Truman to "Mow 'em down, Harry!"

Grinning, the President said, "I'm going to fight hard! I'm going to give them hell!"

"You ought not say 'hell,' " reprimanded Margaret Truman.

Barkley then called out, "It is going to be a victorious trip!"

"Yes, sir!" called back the President, "it's going to be a V—T—!"

September, 1948

". . . if I keep you standing here in this rain any longer you will be against anything I want, and I wouldn't blame you. But I understand that you need the rain worse than you need to listen to any Presidential speech."

Auburn, New York
October 8, 1948

"We can take heart from a comment made by that great American heavyweight champion, Joe Louis. In one fight some time ago he had a hard time catching up with his opponent. But Joe finally did catch up with him, and he knocked him out.

"After the fight, this was what Joe said: 'Well, he could run away, but he couldn't hide.' "

Philadelphia, Pa.
October 6, 1948

"I have a confession to make to you here tonight. For the last two or three weeks I've had a queer feeling that I'm being followed, that someone is following me. I felt it so strongly that I went into consultation with the White House physician. And I told him that I kept having this feeling, that everywhere I go there's somebody following behind me. The White House physician told me not to worry. He said: 'You keep right on your way. There is one place where that fellow is not going to follow you—and that's in the White House.' "

New York City
October 28, 1948

Landing at the Kansas City Airport shortly after the Presidential plane had arrived, a group of reporters rushed to Mr. Truman's home. Much to their surprise, the Presidential party had not yet arrived.

When Mr. Truman finally walked in, he explained:

"We were stopped by a police car and had to pull over. Seems there were some very important people going through town."

October, 1948

Campaigning in Boston, 1948.

The call "Give 'em hell, Harry" became a symbol of President Truman's campaign. When asked how it started, the President said that someone had called it out from the audience during a campaign rally in Seattle, Washington.

"I told him at that time, and I have been repeating it ever since, that I have never deliberately given anybody hell. I just tell the truth on the opposition—and they think it's hell."

"I travelled up and down the country [in 1948]. . . . I kept my eyes open, as well as an ear to the ground, although I remembered what Hanna said about McKinley. He said that he had his ears so close to the ground that he had them full of grasshoppers. But my hearing didn't get impaired."

When a reporter asked President Truman if he thought he would win the election, Mr. Truman retorted:

"Certainly! What do you think I'm running around for?"

October, 1948

The Presidency

1949–1952

President Truman's election was a surprise to many people. To George Allen's frank statement that "I was supremely confident of your defeat," Mr. Truman responded: "So was everybody else. But you're the first one who's admitted it."

Truman answered his own invitation to the 1949 Inauguration in these words:
"Weather permitting, I hope to be present. H.S.T."

At the close of the 1949 Inaugural festivities, the exhausted President quipped:
"It's been a wonderful day. But I'm glad it comes only once every four years."

After delivering a short speech on honesty to a group of students from Colgate University, President Truman pre-

The defeat that turned into victory: A jubilant Harry Truman holds up a newspaper that prematurely awarded the Presidency to his opponent, Thomas E. Dewey.

sented each visitor with a pen on which appeared the inscription: "I swiped this from Harry S. Truman."

February, 1949

When Vice-President Alben Barkley returned from a tour of the South, he found the following note on his desk: "Dear VP: Sorry, I missed you. I needed advice. H.S.T."

April, 1949

"There was an old county judge who was with me on the county court in Jackson County. [He] . . . was a nephew of Senator Money from Mississippi, . . . had been here in Washington with Senator Money, and . . . was a very great philosopher. And he gave me some advice before I left Independence to come to Washington.

"He said, 'Harry, don't you go to the Senate with an inferiority complex. You sit there about six months, and you wonder how you got there. And after that, you wonder how the rest of them got there?' "

Remarks to New Congressmen
April 6, 1949

Alluding to Cato's famous cry: *Delenda est Cathago!* ("Carthage must be destroyed"), President Truman remarked:

"I am happy to say that I have no ill feeling toward these gentlemen who would like to have *delenda est'*ed me."

April, 1949

When Senator Harley M. Kilgore invited the President to join him at a party given by the West Virginia State Society in July, 1949, Mr. Truman shook his head, and said:

"You know I'd love to go, Harley. But they'd only throw five platoons of Secret Service men all over the place. Nobody would have any fun."

July, 1949

At a recital with the National Symphony Orchestra, Margaret Truman was called back for three encores. Singing "Smilin' Through," she looked directly at her parents.

Describing his reaction to the performance, President Truman remarked, "I wept. . . . I almost tore up two programs in the excitement."

September, 1949

When the President was visited by some members of the American Legion's "Girls' Nation," he welcomed them by saying:

"One young lady asked me if in five years she might be an ambassador. I couldn't make her any promises because that is a year or two beyond the time when my term will expire."

September, 1949

Mr. Truman, who is known for his stubbornness, cited a predecessor's opinion about the relationship of President and Cabinet. He pointed out how Abraham Lincoln had once settled a Cabinet dispute: "Well, there's only one deciding vote. The vote is aye."

"There is always a letdown after every war, and the Eightieth Congress was the luckiest thing that ever happened to me."

Mr. Truman sometimes made country-wide trips to gain support for his programs. Addressing a crowd in May, 1950, he said:

"This is a non-political trip. But I may be back later and be a little more interested in politics."

Boarding the Presidential yacht for an overnight rest, Mr. Truman quipped: "The taxpayers are working me too hard."

June, 1950

Private relief bills presented by Senators and Congressmen on behalf of their constituents are usually passed quickly and sent to the President for his signature.

One such bill concerned a California farmer who had lent his horse to the Forest Service. One night, the horse escaped from his stall and accidentally strangled himself with the rope that had been attached to him. The owner

Mr. Truman with the two Bibles he used in his Inaugural ceremony.

applied to the Forest Service for compensation in the amount of one hundred dollars.

When a relief bill granting the farmer seventy-five dollars reached the President's desk, Mr. Truman signed it, and remarked: "A Missouri mule would not have been fool enough to get himself choked to death."

October, 1950

When President Truman vetoed the Basing Point Bill of 1950, after waiting till the end of the ten-day grace period, a Congressman asked if it had been difficult for him to make up his mind.

"I intended to veto it all along," answered Mr. Truman. "In fact, I feel like the blacksmith on the Missouri jury. The judge asked if he was prejudiced against the defendant.

" 'Oh, no, Judge. I think we ought to give him a fair trial. Then I think we ought to take the s.o.b. out and string him up.' "

"I was reading a story in one of the papers the other day where a man had called the doctor about three o'clock in the morning and said that his wife had appendicitis and that he wished the doctor would come immediately and do something about it.

"The doctor told the man to give his wife bicarbonate of soda—that he knew very well that she didn't have two appendixes, as he had taken one out just three years before.

"The man came back with the statement that he knew

**The President in one of the gaudy
sport shirts for which he became
famous.**

a woman couldn't have two appendixes but a man could have two wives in three years."

During a conference in October, 1950, Douglas MacArthur took out his pipe, turned courteously to the President, and asked him if he minded the smoke.

"No," answered the President, "I suppose I have had more smoke blown at me than any other man alive."

Noting the vast array of battle decorations and campaign ribbons worn at the 72nd Conference of the National Guard Association in 1950, President Truman remarked:

"I wish I could sport some of them. About all I ever receive . . . [are] the bricks. It's a good thing I have got a pretty hard head, or it would have been broken a long time ago."

Exchanging ideas with a group of 4H members, Mr. Truman commented:

"I hope to go back to the farm some day. Some people are in a hurry for me to go back, but I'm not going back as fast as they want me to."

January, 1951

At a dinner he gave for twenty-one freshmen Democrats of the House of Representatives in January, 1951, Mr. Truman had this to say about the Presidency:

"There is one thing about this job. It has no future to it. Every young man wants something to look forward to."

Alluding to his daughter's growing fame as a singer, President Truman quipped to a crowd in Ohio in 1951:

"I would like all you people to meet Margaret Truman's father. . . . I'm a back number already."

At the 73rd Conference of the National Guard Association, President Truman reminisced about his first experience as a member of the National Guard. He explained how, at the age of twenty-one dressed in a handsome blue uniform with "red stripes down the britches," he proudly walked into the room where his old grandmother, Mrs. Solomon Young, was seated.

Mrs. Young's farm had been ransacked by Federal soldiers during the Civil War, and when she saw her grandson, she said sharply: "Harry, that's the first time since 1865 a blue uniform has been in my house. Don't bring it here anymore."

November, 1951

Fiercely loyal to his state of Missouri, which John Gunther has called "the crossroads of the nation," Mr. Truman, visited by the famous author, pointed to the state on a map and maintained that Missouri was the only state in the Union which could get along even if a fence were built around it.

Turning to Mr. Gunther, he added laughingly, "And Missourians are ornery folks—against everybody."

Mr. Gunther asked pointedly, "What are they *for*?"

"Missouri," Mr. Truman happily replied.

In December, 1951, the President interrupted a much-needed vacation in Key West, Florida, to attend a dinner given by the Women's National Democratic Club.

"Mrs. Truman made this engagement for the two of us," he remarked, "and when I have a date with Mrs. Truman, I usually keep it."

With Vice-President Barkley.

President Truman dashed the familiar legend that George Washington had thrown a silver dollar across the Potomac River.

"It was a Spanish piece of eight," protested the President, "and it was thrown across the Rappahannock. Any ten-year-old boy could throw a dime across at that place. But I am doubtful that Washington, with his acquisitive habits, would even let loose a Spanish piece of eight."

November, 1951

When Dwight D. Eisenhower was running for President, Mr. Truman told his aides what he thought about having a general elected to the office of Chief Executive:

"He'll sit right here, and he'll say, 'Do this! Do that!'

And nothing will happen. Poor Ike—it won't be a bit like the army. He'll find it very frustrating."

November, 1952

While Mr. Truman was preparing to vacate the White House in January, 1953, he remarked to visiting Senator Harley M. Kilgore:

"If I had known there would be so much work leaving this place, I'd have run again."

January, 1953

En route to his Inauguration, Dwight D. Eisenhower turned to the outgoing President, and asked: "I wonder who is responsible for my son John being ordered to Washington from Korea? I wonder who is trying to embarrass me?"

"The President of the United States ordered your son to attend your Inauguration," replied Mr. Truman. "If you think somebody was trying to embarrass you by this order, then the President assumes full responsibility."

January 20, 1953

The Press Conferences

Two days after Japan had announced its surrender, the President called a press conference "... because I thought you hadn't all had a chance to look me in the face or ask me any impertinent questions. I haven't anything that you would break your arms to get out of the door for this morning....

"I have issued a proclamation setting aside Sunday as a day of prayer. After the two-days' celebration [of Japan's unconditional surrender] I think we will need the prayer."

August 16, 1945

Question: "Mr. President, this morning's *Post* has an editorial saying it thinks you ought to appoint a lot of Republicans ..."

President Truman: "I'm a Democrat."

September 12, 1945

Question: "What kind of music do you like best?"

President Truman: "I am very fond of piano music, particularly. I like Chopin, Mozart, and Beethoven. I am very fond of Gilbert and Sullivan operas, and Verdi operas. Most any kind of music I like, except noise. I don't like noise."

April 6, 1946

Question: "Mr. President, have you read Walter Lippmann's articles on Germany?"

President Truman: "Yes, I have read them."

Question: "Would you care to comment on them?"

President Truman: "Well, as I commented at the Gridiron dinner: hindsight is a great thing."

May 9, 1946

Question: "Mr. President, the *New York Times* this morning has a story out of Paris saying that there is—may be—a drastic change in our foreign policy regarding Russia, inasmuch as Russia has not cooperated in the various fields. Is there anything you could say on that?"

President Truman: "No. I haven't heard about it, and I make the policy."

May 9, 1946

Question: "Mr. President, do you have any plans to seize the Pittsburgh ball club?"

President Truman: "The Pittsburgh ball club goes on strike?"

Question: "They are going to go out tomorrow night."

President Truman: "Well, I want to say to you that if those ball fellows go on strike, and I have to take them over, I'll have two damn good teams in St. Louis."

June 6, 1946

Question: "Mr. President, the Republican national campaign director today accuses you of ingannation in connection with your budget."

President Truman: "Well, I guess that's just to add to the obfuscation of all the rest of his statement. That's about in line with what he's trying to say."

Question: "Mr. President, getting back to the ingannation — "

President Truman: "The obfuscation."

Question: "Get him to spell that, will you?"

President Truman: "Well, I will spell it for you. I had it looked up in the dictionary. It means deceit or deception, and it is spelled i-n-g-a-n-n-a-t-i-o-n. I don't use $40 words like that in my language."

Question: "Is that a double *n*, Mr. President?"

President Truman: "That's a Republican word. It isn't Democratic."

August 9, 1946

Question: "Mr. President, you said you hadn't made any advance calculations or bets on the elections. Are you willing to lay a small wager?"

An informal news conference on the lawn of the "little White House" in Key West, Florida.

President Truman: "It's contrary to the law in the state of Missouri to make a bet on the election. I expect to vote in the state of Missouri."

October 24, 1946

"Well, I am glad to see you this morning [May 8, 1947]. Just two years ago I called you in here at 8:30 in the morning and made an announcement that the Germans had surrendered officially, and read you two proclamations, I think: one calling for a day of prayer the following Sunday, and one outlining the necessity for continued work until the Japanese had surrendered. There was a grand rush after that announcement was made, and Merriman Smith broke his arm as he went out the door, and another fellow here broke his leg—almost but not quite. . . . So I hope there won't be any occasion for such a tremendous rush this morning. . . ."

President Truman proceeded to discuss the major international events and peace programs of the period since the end of the war.

Question: "Mr. President, how old do you feel today, in view of all that?"

President Truman: "Oh, about the same as I did when I came to the Senate in 1935."

These remarks were made to members of the Association of Radio News Analysts:

"Well, it's good to have you here. As I told you all on

several occasions, there is nothing that I can tell you. You are always telling *me* what to do!

"Very frankly, I think every one of you has given me the right advice on Greece and Turkey, internal affairs and foreign affairs and taxes, and this portal-to-portal, and the labor bill.

"If I don't get those things right, I can assure you, gentlemen, it won't be *your* fault!"

May 13, 1947

Question: "Mr. President, have you seen any flying saucers?"

President Truman: "Only in the newspapers."

July 10, 1947

Question: "For the whole valley? You said you are for the Missouri Valley Authority plan?"

President Truman: "I think I have said it a dozen times. You want me to put it down in writing and hand it to you?"

July 10, 1947

Question: "Mr. President, there has been some printed speculation that Dr. Steelman* might leave your personal staff and head the new Federal Conciliation Service. Would you care to comment on that?"

President Truman: "I hadn't heard about it, and I don't think Dr. Steelman has, either. I think he is pretty well satisfied working twenty-four hours a day for me."

July 10, 1947

*John Steelman, special assistant to the President.

"I have just been reading a book by a fellow named Pollard—*Presidents and the Press*!

"When you read what the press had to say about Washington, Jefferson, and Lincoln, and the other Presidents, you would think that we never had a decent man in the office since the country began."

April 23, 1948

"I invited Stalin to come to Washington, and he said, 'God willing, I will come.' Well, I haven't met anybody yet who believes me, but that is what he said to me."

April, 1948

Question: "Mr. President, did Dr. Weizmann suggest a loan to Israel?"

President Truman: "He did not suggest a loan. He said he would like to have a loan, just like every other country. If you know of any countries that wouldn't like to have a loan, I wish you would name them."

May 27, 1948

Question: "Mr. President, Senator McGrath predicts that you will be nominated on the first ballot in Philadelphia. . . ."

President Truman: "Mr. McGrath is correct."

July, 1948

Question: "Mr. President, Mr. Dewey [the 1948 Republican Presidential candidate] was lamenting the fact that the Republican party is split wide open. Do you have any advice for him that would — "

President Truman: "I gave him all the advice I possibly could during the campaign."

February 10, 1949

On one particularly difficult day someone handed the President the following statement, which he smilingly shared with the assembled newsmen:

"Things seem to be going fairly well. A spirit of pessimism prevails in all departments."

Harry Truman's Mother

As a young girl, Martha Ellen Truman, the President's mother, attended the Baptist College for Women in Lexington, Missouri. Laughingly flaunting Baptist decrees against dancing, she commented, "I'm a lightfoot Baptist."

Mr. and Mrs. Truman had known each other since early childhood. They became engaged during World War I and were married on June 28, 1919. Mr. Truman's mother was once asked why her son Harry did not marry until he was thirty-five years of age.

"Maybe she wouldn't have him before then," she replied.

After Harry Truman was nominated for the Vice-Presidency at the 1944 Democratic Convention, his cousin, General Ralph E. Truman, remarked to the nominee's mother that she must be very proud of her son. "Oh, well," she answered with a smile, "I liked him just as well before."

Mrs. Truman, who had listened carefully to the proceedings of the Convention, commented, "We were just blessing off old Texas because the Texas delegates didn't give all the votes to Harry. I don't see why Texas would vote for anyone from Iowa."

After the election, Mrs. Truman asserted:
"That boy could plow the straightest row of corn in the whole county. He was a farmer who could do everything there was to do just a little better than anyone else."

As soon as he was sworn in as Vice-President, Harry Truman phoned his mother:
"Did you hear it on the radio?" he asked.
"Yes, I heard it all," she said. 'Now you behave yourself up there, Harry. Now you behave yourself!"
"I will, Mamma," he promised.

When Mr. Truman became President, Mrs. Truman remarked:
"I can't really be glad he is President, because I'm sorry that the President [Roosevelt] is dead. If he had been voted in, I'd be out waving a flag; but it doesn't seem right to be very happy or wave a flag now."

Mr. Truman and his mother.

When the official thirty-day period of mourning for President Franklin D. Roosevelt was over, Mr. Truman sent the Presidential airplane *Sacred Cow* to bring his mother and sister to Washington to celebrate Mother's Day. It was Mrs. Truman's first experience on a plane, and while she was being helped out of the aircraft, the elevator, which had been specially installed for use by the late President, got stuck.

Turning to the pilot, Mrs. Truman said: "I am going to tell Harry that this plane is no good, and [that] I could walk just as easily as I could ride."

May, 1945

Martha Truman was very much concerned about the bed she was to occupy while visiting the White House. Her son Vivian had told her that she would be sleeping in the Lincoln Room, in the bed Lincoln had used.

Unhappy about the arrangement, she said to Vivian, "You tell Harry, if he puts me in the room with Lincoln's bed in it, I'll sleep on the floor."

May, 1945

In her nineties, Mrs. Truman once advised her son: "You be good, but be game, too."

September 24, 1945

The President's concern for his mother's health lessened whenever she began discussing politics. It was always an indication that she was regaining her strength. In 1947, Mrs. Truman asked her son whether Senator Robert Taft was going to be nominated for President.

Young Harry Truman in the uniform of the Missouri State Guard.

"He might be," answered Mr. Truman.

"Harry, are you going to run?" asked Mrs. Truman, looking sharply at her son.

"I don't know, Mamma," he replied.

"Don't you think it's about time you made up your mind?"

Martha Truman was raised in Missouri, which had been a buffer state between the Confederates and the Union. Sympathetic tendencies to the Southern cause may well be reflected in an incident which occurred when, at age ninety-two, she broke her hip.

Her son came to visit her and found her in bed, bandaged. Before the President could voice his concern, his mother snapped, "I don't want any smart cracks out of you. I saw your picture in the paper last week putting a wreath at the Lincoln Memorial!"

"I'm not a giggly woman, but I can't help smiling when people cheer at the mention of Harry's name."

March, 1947

During Mrs. Truman's last illness, L. Curtis Tiernan, former chaplain of Battery "D" (in which the President served during World War I), paid her a visit.

"Mrs. Truman," he said, "you must be very proud that a son of yours is in the White House."

"Well, yes," she answered, "but I have got another son who lives down the road a piece—and I'm just as proud of him."

Private Citizen

As soon as the inaugural ceremonies for Dwight D. Eisenhower were over, President and Mrs. Truman drove to Union Station to board the train for Independence, Missouri.

Feeling a greater measure of freedom than he had for many years, Mr. Truman walked through the train, often startling the passengers, who were unaccustomed to seeing the President of the United States unescorted.

He stopped at a Pullman compartment, opened the door, and stuck his head in. When the occupants did not recognize him, he turned and said happily, "Things are getting back to normal when that happens."

January, 1953

Upon their return to Independence, in January, 1953, the Trumans were warmly and royally greeted by friends and neighbors.

Mr. Truman acknowledged the cordiality by saying,

"After I get finished with the job Mrs. Truman has for me —unpacking—I'll be open for dinner engagements. I may be hungry—I don't have a job."

A chauffeur once drove the Trumans to the neighborhood they were visiting, but stopped at the wrong house. When Mr. Truman rang the bell, an "unmistakably Republican-looking gentleman opened the door." The error became apparent at once.

"I hope your feelings won't be hurt," said the man, staring intently, "but you look exactly like Harry Truman."

"I hope yours won't be either," was the reply, "but I *am* Harry Truman."

Mrs. Truman once reminded her husband that the grass around their house needed to be trimmed. Mr. Truman neglected the matter until one Sunday morning, when he took out the lawn mower and started to work as neighbors passed by on their way to church.

Horror-stricken, Mrs. Truman rushed out to protest that cutting the grass was hardly the right thing to be doing on Sunday.

"I'm doing what you asked me to do," Mr. Truman reminded her. Later, he recalled that "the neighbors continued to pass by the house. Their glances were not lost on Mrs. Truman. She never asked me to mow the lawn again."

One morning, Mr. Truman, gliding out of his narrow driveway, cringed as he heard the crunch of chrome and paint being scratched away from the side of his new car.

He decided to say nothing of this to his wife, and he continued on to his appointment.

A few days later, Mrs. Truman telephoned him to explain, hesitatingly and haltingly, that she had just had a little accident. While driving out of the narrow driveway, she had scratched off the chrome and paint from the side of her new car!

Neither ever made any further mention of the experience.

When Bess Truman was about to burn the letters he had written to her, the President protested:

"You oughtn't do that."

"Why not?" asked Mrs. Truman. "I've read them several times."

"But think of history!" her husband exhorted.

"I have!"

On a nationally televised production of the "Person to Person" program for which Margaret Truman substituted for Edward R. Murrow as interviewer, Mr. Truman answered one of his daughter's questions with these remarks:

". . . the fence [around the Truman home in Independence] had to be put up to offset the American propensities for collecting souvenirs and tearing the house down. I was told that when Herbert Hoover went to Washington as President, they took the doorknobs off his house and almost tore the house down, and that was done before they placed the guards there to prevent it. The Secret Service decided that the fence would save our property from being destroyed.

"It is an old story that Americans like to collect souvenirs. When I was in the First World War it was said that the British fought for the control of the seas, the French for the freedom of France, and the Americans fought for souvenirs. And they are still fighting for them."

The Trumans flew into New York and were met at Kennedy Airport by their daughter and her husband, Clifton Daniels.

Asked about the length of his visit, Mr. Truman said: "I'll be here for six days, or until my son-in-law gets tired of me."

August 16, 1965

A young girl visiting the Truman Library asked Mr. Truman if he had considered running for office again.

"Well, I could," he answered. "The Twenty-second Amendment, which limits the President to two terms, doesn't apply to me, so there's nothing to stop me from running again if I wanted to. . . .

"I've said that I'm going to run again for President when I'm ninety. You know, some fools took me seriously and looked into that and said I couldn't run when I'm ninety because there's no election that year. . . ."

The remark that the President's father, John Anderson Truman, had been a failure in life, drew this retort:

"My father was not a failure. After all, he was the father of a President of the United States."

Mr. Truman has often been asked what his middle initial stands for. He explains that since both his grandfathers' names began with "S," his parents decided to designate his middle name with that letter, thus allowing each side of the family to assume that they were being honored.

"Missouri has produced three notorious characters— Mark Twain, Jesse James, and me. Mark and Jesse are dead, but I'm still here filling in for them."

"I never really cared much for the "Missouri Waltz." My favorite waltzes are ones by Chopin, but my piano playing stopped long ago. A lot of people think that if I'd gone ahead and been a music hall pianist, the country would have been a lot better off."

Asked whether he could play poker, Mr. Truman commented:

"I have played a game where you put the first card face down and the others face up. Then everybody bets, and you turn your hold card up—and somebody takes the money."

"I learned to play poker in France—but it was a costly education."

Mr. Truman explained that he had stopped trying to grow a beard because "the hair on the right side of my face grew upward, and on the left side it grew down."

A school boy asked Mr. Truman to describe the difference between Democrats and Republicans.

"Democrats work to help people who need help," he explained. "That other party, they work for people who don't need help. That's all there's to it."

"Then how come so many Republicans are elected to office?" the boy asked.

"Because they had the most votes!" Mr. Truman said, smiling.

In 1960, Mr. Truman was not convinced that John F. Kennedy was ready for the Presidency. His concern was not Kennedy's religion but rather his lack of administrative experience and the possibility of his father's strong influence:

"It's not the Pope who worries me, it's the Pop."

Reports were widely circulated that Senator Robert F. Kennedy was carefully laying plans for the Presidential nomination in 1972.

Asked his opinion, Mr. Truman looked into his political crystal ball and forecast with assurance that Vice-President Hubert Humphrey would be the nominee in 1972.

"And that's not a prediction," he added. "That's a fact."

December 23, 1965

A champion of the common man, Mr. Truman has always had little time or patience for those who rest their laurels on ancestral claim.

Once asked what he thought of those who call them-

Mr. Truman plays for President and Mrs. Kennedy at the White House in 1961. Behind him is pianist Eugene List.

selves one-hundred-percent Americans, he told the following story.

Will Rogers was once speaking before members of the Daughters of the American Revolution, and he noted that they were wearing badges indicating that their forefathers had come to America in the days of the Pilgrims, or before. He commended them for their glory, and smiles of pride and contentment broke out on the nodding faces.

Rogers went on to boast of his ancestors, reminding the audience that his own forefathers were on the shores of America to greet the first immigrants. Will Rogers, Mr. Truman pointed out, was part Indian.

Mr. Truman's lifelong habit of taking a brisk morning walk has become a trademark. He has kept many an interviewer panting after him.

Visiting in New York, in December, 1965, Mr. Truman scheduled an early-morning interview with newsmen. He appeared in the lobby of his hotel at the appointed time, and headed for the street.

When the reporters suggested that he conduct his interview in the warm lobby, Mr. Truman, undaunted, continued out and smilingly nudged the group on with the remark, "It'll do you good!"

When reporters asked what Christmas gifts he was giving to his grandchildren, Mr. Truman responded cagily, "I'm not going to tell you because they would hear it on the radio. They listen all day long."